Woman

an autobiographical book of poetry

Karrine Steffans

ISBN-10: 0615718779
ISBN-13: 978-0615718774

Dedication

For Abuelo...

And So It Began

I was a babe with the weight of the world upon my shoulders and the concerns of adults swirling through my head. It kept me up nights as I lie in my bed — upon the top bunk. Below me was my sister, seven years younger, and just a few feet away was my mother's bed where she slept with our youngest sister, just born.

I was nine years old and had already fallen in love and been swept away, day after day, for years. I was just five when I stumbled upon an old book in the library of my school in St. Thomas. These Virgin Islands, though just thirty miles wide, were rich in culture and steeped in the importance of learnedness. As I parted its pages, the spine crackled and a light flurry of dust escaped its crevice. It smelled of years passed with a sturdy cover, its jacket long lost, and tender, water stained pages.

I sat upon the floor in my uniform, my dark brown, pleated skirt defying the dirt, the pocket of my yellow, button-down shirt telling on the pounding of my heart. I was drawn to him, the man who wrote these words, and felt I'd found a place to escape where I was understood. He wrote, *Once upon a midnight dreary, while I pondered, weak*

*and weary, over a many quaint and
curious volume of forgotten lore...*

I loved him, then.

I took home that book filled with
the complete tales and poetry of Edgar
Allan Poe and read and read, devouring
his syntax, delighting in the way he let
the words flutter and play. They had
movement and I could see them
dancing before me, intertwined,
intermingled, inviting me to twirl with
them and, so, I did.

I began writing.

It must have been the summer of
that same year when my mother took
me to New York where my father was
born and lived. Also living there was my
grandfather whom I, affectionately,
called, Abuelo. Part Puerto Rican, part
Dane, I remember him as a slightly

portly man, but I have never been sure if this was his actual build of just the way I saw him as a little girl — big, soft, and comforting. He lived in Brooklyn, just steps away from where he worked and, during my time with him, he would make me Spam sandwiches and hold my hand as we walked to his office. On the way, Abuelo always stopped for a copy of the *New York Times*.

The office smelled of mildew and in the vacant lot next to it, there was a team of construction workers erecting a new building. The noise was unnerving and I could never understand how my grandfather and the other men in the office could get any work done, there. I would look out the window next to Abuelo's desk and watch the men jackhammer, dig, and rivet. Abuelo would read his paper with a mug of coffee.

Peeping over his rounded shoulders, I discovered a list. It was just a list, lying there on the page. "Abuelo, what's that?" I asked, pointing over his shoulder.

"That's the best sellers list. It's where all the best writers go," he answered, before closing his paper and flinging it open to a new page. "Keep reading and writing like you do and, one day, you'll be on that list, too!"

I would never forget that day and what Abuelo said and even though I didn't really understand the concept, I just knew I had to get there — to that list.

Lying in that top bunk, years later, I would recite Poe's poetry in my head and create my own prose, eager for the sun to rise so I could climb down from my bed and write it all down. And, so, I did. I wrote poetry almost every day for years, every bit of it autobiographical, every line coming from something deep inside of me. And I never forgot Poe, even when I discovered others like Angelou and Thoreau.

Twenty years after Abuelo introduced me to the *New York Times* best sellers list and projected I would, one day, be *on* that list, I was. My first book, *Confessions of a Video Vixen* was published in 2005, entered the list at number seven, peaked at number five, and stayed on the list for over twenty-two weeks. My second and third books would also make the list.

As chronicled in *Confessions*, my life had always been tough but, through it all, I wrote poetry. Crushingly, all the poetry I'd written as a girl was thrown away as I bounced from house to house as a teenage runaway. It killed me to have lost it all and, for years, I had not written a stitch of prose. Then, suddenly, during one of the darkest periods of my life, I was inspired and began to write again. It was 1996 and, though I would never write poetry as often as I had as a child, I wrote often for a time. Over the next ten years, I'd doodle a little and make things rhyme, yet, I was never possessed with the overwhelming need to write poetry, again.

I tucked a few pieces of poetry away and forgot.

Then, the worst thing that could happen to a writer, happened to me. With the publishing and success of my books came the machine that sucked the love of writing from my marrow. I became a cog. When the time came to write my fourth book, *SatisFaction*, I couldn't. It wasn't mine. My editor chose its title, the cover, and the subject matter and I paid someone else to write it.

I'd lost my love.

I lay in bed for years, caught in a cloud of blackness with no sight of day. I couldn't think of what to write, how to write, or even if anyone wanted me to. My passion had fled as what started as a form of breathing began to stifle me and I began to doubt my gift in its entirety. I'd submitted a dozen ideas to my editor before she denied them all and left the company. I felt abandoned, pushed aside. As the industry began to crumble with the advent and explosion of the digital download, which dominated and changed the landscape of the industry, budgets shrunk. There was no money for marketing and my sales dwindled, then, plummeted. My love of the art had become nothing but a business and business was suffering.

I was suffering.

In 2011, I began to come alive again and dabble with a few book ideas but never regained the confidence to complete a project. Nothing was good enough. I wasn't good enough. I'd made it through a series of harrowing personal defeats and was on my way to rebuilding my life, personally and professionally.

Still, no inspiration.

By year's end, I'd decided to nurture the inspiration of others and start publishing a collection of anthologies written by and for my readers. I switched hats and turned from writer to publisher and editor. It was the perfect distraction from my failed inspiration and a way to dip my toes back into the pool of publishing but, this time, on my grounds. Meanwhile, I continued to dabble, but nothing I wrote gave me joy. With our first anthology, *Drink Fuck Sleep*, on the verge of being published and our second, *The Secret Life of Sugar*, well underway, Steffans Publishing was fulfilling its promise to its writers, but I, its chief, was still without direction. In the interim, I'd garnered two development deals with Fox Television

Studios when they optioned *Confessions of a Video Vixen* and, my third book, *The Vixen Manual: How to Find, Seduce, & Keep the Man You Want* and began writing and executive producing these projects for television. I was thrilled to be expanding my writing portfolio but desperately missed standing at my ground zero.

Then came a film.

It was April 27, 2012 when I walked into the theatre with my teenage son to see *Raven*, a fictional thriller built upon the works of Poe, played by John Cusak. I'd introduce my son to Poe the year before and he, too, found the author mesmerizing. As the script intermingled Poe's work with the deviant malice of a serial killer and offered an entertaining spin on the author's death, I found myself becoming inspired. The film brought to my remembrance the depth of his works and my original love of them and all things poetry. I remembered the lot of poems I'd tucked away years before and, all of a sudden, I wanted to write, again. I gasped and covered my gaping jaw as the film centered on the Danish Virgin Islands, showing a map of St. Croix, St. Thomas, and St. John. I whispered, "Abuelo."

So, I rushed home and dug up these poems, read them over, and cried as it all came rushing back to me. And this is where I start. At the beginning. I never meant for anyone to read these poems and I was always told by publishers poetry would never sell. Today, none of that matters. What follows are poems written between 1995 and 2005 and are presented in alphabetical ordering. They all represent a period of time in my life and a few were written for people I have loved and lost. Of all my writing, these are the most intimate and I am proud to share them with you.

I have been inspired.

- Karrine

A Thousand

A thousand deaths
I count today,
Of a thousand loves
Buried someplace far away.
Long ago,
Still a thousand memories
Flood this broken shell,
Pouring out as ink to these lines;
A thousand words I know well.
A thousand nights
Carry on into days
Where emptiness sleeps,
Awakens and stays.
A thousand poisoned tears
Burn my satin face and lips,
Scorching the reminiscence
Of your misplaced kiss.
I know no place,
I know no time or space;
Just a thousand ways
Times a thousand ways.

All the Times

For all the times
I sat before
A paper and pen to write.
For all the days
This was all I had
Even after they turned to nights.
I write these words,
Not knowing how;
It's been years and I've forgotten.
Now, I wish
To ripen this fruit gone bad,
That my soul has hollowed rotten.
I find a love
Within these words
That I have known since I was young.
And, in these lines,
I still can see,
My heroes yet unsung.
With every hurt
And scattered joy
I could always fight with script.
Those days long gone,
I lost my strength
And sealed my solemn crypt.
Could it be back,
I only wonder;

Have I, somehow, been inspired
To give my pen,
Some soul again,
With a wit I thought retired?
Well, for what it's worth,
Here it is,
It's all I could think to say
About this girl,
Somehow, reborn
Here on this page, today.
And for all the memories
I used to know,
They'll never compare to this.
Finding a love I thought was gone,
Not knowing it still exists.

Already

Within my sorrow
There rises the sun,
As my forever
Becomes tomorrow,
And my accomplishments, done.
A draft fills this room
And whistles a sweet song,
That I may sleep through the end,
Wondering why
This doesn't seem wrong.
That I lay here this dawn,
Overcome by my meekness,
Damp and dark.
Waiting for a sign,
For death to leave his mark.
How will I know him
Apart from this place?
With his flesh cold as mine
And his, identical to my face.
Pondering over the last,
To some,
Might sound so petty.
I accept no condolences,
For I
Am death,
Already.

Always Never

Always chasing,
But never finding
Exactly what I need.
So, in my mind
I begin to wonder,
If it *actually* exists, indeed.
What I do find, however,
Are falsities;
Things that do not exist.
And, in my heart,
I cry so hard;
Nothing's as depressing as this.
Hopeless, maybe.
Maybe that's the word
That best describes this chase.
But, for sure, it's anguish
And painful failure
That appear upon my face.
I'm always chasing,
Always losing,
Always incomplete.
Never finding,
Never winning,
Never accepting defeat.

Angel

Once in your lifetime,
You'll come across an angel
And he will be your biggest blessing.
He will comfort your fears,
He will bring you joy,
And truth for your soul's confessing.
This angel will help you,
He will hold your hand,
And take you where you haven't gone.
He will hover over
Each waking hour
Between your dusk and your dawn.
And, though, he's physically
Distant at times,
He's never really far off hand.
And when you speak
With an honest tongue,
He will never judge
But he will understand.
To him,
There is no beginning
And there is no end,
For before you even knew him
He was already your friend.
You ask how I know

And my answer is uncommon but true.
I have seen this angel,
He is a part of me,
And, to me,
That angel is you.

Anyway

And where were you anyway
When I was in need?
All I felt was despair
Forsaken and alone, indeed.
Where were you, then,
And as my soul cried out?
Were you around?
Somewhere roaming about?
Wasn't I one?
Solitaire?
But you wouldn't know.
You
Weren't even there.
Where ever you were, then?
Just look where I am, now.
I don't care what the reason,
I don't want to know how.
Because, now, I have moved on
And I, too, have gone away.
So, I don't care where you were,
Or who you are,
Anyway.

As Sure As I Breathe

As sure as I breathe,
I wish I would not.
As quickly as my heart beats,
I wish it would stop.
For I cannot understand
The power of this,
Of your touch against mine,
Your embrace,
Your kiss.
And, though, there have been others,
They do not compare to you.
And, although, I have lied to them,
To you, I have been true.
There are no mistakes,
Though, I cannot explain my heart.
Why I cry at our finish,
Before our very start.
As sure as I breathe,
I wish I would not,
If you cannot breathe with me,
If my touch you forgot.
As quickly as my heart beats,
I wish it would not,
If yours beats not with mine,
If your heart's turned cold,
When once it burned hot.

I ache so immensely
I cannot sleep.
I cry while I dream
For my devotion runs deep.
And I hate myself
For the way I feel,
And hate myself more
In the realization the emotion is real.
Ignore me, if you wish,
Never answer my call,
Never wonder about me,
Never catch me when I fall.
Still, this is a testament,
To the verses in my heart.
For you are in my blood,
Which stands still
When we're apart.
As sure as I breathe,
As quickly as my heart beats,
I still wish they would stop.
And I wish I were yours,
And you wish I were not.

Before

Picture me here,
If you can see
In the dark.
Just me in this chair,
Baring death's mark.
It squeaks beneath me
As I rock to and fro,
Between nothing
And nowhere,
No one to know.
Thank you for coming
And listening to this,
To the sounds
Of confinement,
Solitary abyss.
Close the door
Behind you,
You'll let the spirits go.
Lost souls
Are confined, too,
Each of them,
I know.
They play with the shadows
Of times
Already passed,
And dance to a tune

They can hear,
At last.
Come closer.
Let me see you
Before I go on.
Lend me your ear,
I only have until dawn.
You're afraid of this place,
For the stench
In the air,
For the mice
At your feet,
For the weight
Of my stare.
You're repulsed
By the manner
In which I live,
When, in fact,
It is death
That does not forgive.
Nothing surrounds me,
Nothing in the least.
A night stand
By my chair,
A glass of water,
My feast;
That which is thirsty,
Rye bread
Tends to starve,
The chill nips my toes,

Scratching the floor,
They tend to carve.
A candle
Flickers its last,
As does my existence.
As my wick burns shorter
I apply no resistance.
For my chest
Has been hollowed
And my heart
Beats faintly within.
I am reminiscent
Of my younger days,
Reckless acts of sin.
I long so
To be like you,
Overcome
By the time.
Youth is gone
And all I have
Are barrens
To call mine.
Grasp my hand,
Let the feel of ice
Chill you to the bone.
Listen to
My inner peace
And my wary spirit moan.
I tremble so,
And slur these words;

I tend to feel misplaced.
I'll say it now,
Before I go,
Necessity accompanies haste.
So, as the wind
Whistles through
All the crevices throughout,
The clock
Ticks in tune
As time proceeds
With doubt.
Look inside,
Look beyond,
Look behind the gore.
For you are me
Just the way
I was you,
Before.

Believe

Nobody knows
Just how alone,
Just how sad
I am,
That I spend
Every week's end
In a dark, still room,
My whole life,
A sham.
The smiles
And laughter,
The charade
Of the actress within,
Left alone
After all the nights
Turned into days of sin.
They believe
That I am happy
And that I have
So much,
That my life is full
And there are people
Close enough to touch.
They believe in the stories
Told to them

By other believers,
They believe in the things
That even I have said,
For I am one
Of the great deceivers.
I walk around this town
All alone,
With really nowhere to go,
I hope that someone will see me
And make my stalled life,
Go.
I hope for someone to catch my eye
And make me
Feel again,
Something new
Rather than thinking
Of my happiness
Way back when.
I am all alone
And I have few reasons,
No new life,
No new seasons.
So, while they all are changing,
I stay the same.
All alone,
Believing this pain.

Can't Find the Words

I can't find the words;
Between my heart and mouth
They are lost.
I can't tell this pain,
For I'm not sure what will be the cost.
In poetic form
It sounds so sweet,
For the melody drowns the sorrow.
But bitter, still,
Are the taste of the tears
I awake with every tomorrow.
I pray for a release
And my deliverance soon,
For I fear my will to die.
Inside it hurts
As I begin to crumble
And with every breath,
I cry.
I can't find the words,
I really can't,
For this is, simply, residue.
But, one day, you will see
A bigger, better me,
And I will no longer be you.

Forgive Me Not

Forget me not
When I am born
A time not yet of yours.
Let me grow
Within myself
To, in your world,
Open doors.
Forever within
My eyesight see
Nothing
More than what is me.
Let me out
Of caged existence
Into lighter days.
Show me myself
For my precious being,
Loving and tender ways.
What do I say,
For I only babble
I guess to satisfy the need.
To be heard aloud ,
Clear as day
For myself,
Alone and indeed.

Fortunato

Forgive me now,
Fortune's fool,
Where self is often foe.
Where am I?
Who can I be?
By the graces,
Fortunato.
Inside a cell
Within mine eyes,
Myself,
Embraced in sorrow.
By what means?
Reasons why.
Pronounce me,
Fortunato.
Mask thy face,
Who is ashamed,
And be
What you do not know.
For I, myself,
Am inside of me,
In the heart
Of Fortunato.
What's in a name?
It sounds unlikely,
Proud to say it is so.

For in every curse,
There is me,
This fool,
This Fortunato.
Forgive me now,
Fortune's fool,
This from head to toe.
I know myself
Apart from you
Doomed
Is Fortunato.

Four Twenty

No one cold have told me
My life could be changed
The way that it has and will.

I could not have imagined
That such a love would bloom
On the twentieth day of April.

For all the things
That I've been through,
I swore my heart
Could take no more.

But changed my mind
One brisk spring night
On that day
Of month number four.

I have forgotten it all,
The days before
The evening that we met.
And all my memories seem to be
Of things
That haven't happened, yet.

So here's to us and our love

And to promises of more,
To growing and sharing,
Celebrating each year,
The twentieth day
Of month number four.

Hello

Hello
To the days
Far behind.
To the time
On my clock,
Rewind.
To the laughter
To which
I am faithfully
Bound.
A song
To sing,
That day
That sound.
Hello.
I have missed
Your touch
In time.
Forever a part
Of me,
Of mine.
Heart and soul,
Pieces of a whole,
You
Keep it all
Together.

I think
Of you
Whenever
I need to know
What's gone
Is back
To say
Hello.

How It Feels

Do you know how it feels
To loose sight of yourself
And begin to wither away?
Do you know how it feels
To watch yourself go
But wishing that you could stay?
When there is nothing you can do
To reverse the pull
That drives you so very far.
Do you know how it feels
To not know where you'll be
In a life that's so bizarre?
Believe when I say
I know the feeling
And it tears away at your heart.
Watching you and yourself
Go separate ways
Not knowing why you part.
Existing in the moment
Knowing it can change,
Dragging behind life's heels.
Ask me just once,
Show me you care,
And I will tell you
How it feels.

Let Go

Behind this strength
You'll find a heart
Not willing
To let go.
That memory,
Inside of me,
Some days
That's all I know.
I live on this,
It's what I breathe,
The only drink,
To cure my thirst.
I live in bliss,
It's all I need,
It's what I think of,
Last and first.
Don't bother me
With moving on,
I am in a good place.
You couldn't believe
Or understand
Those days,
Their smell,
Their taste.
I'm happy there

In that time,
Where there was so much space to
grow.
And still, to this day,
I tend to return,
Not willing
To let go.

Necessity

Out of necessity
Of a place to hide,
I give you these words
From a hollow place inside.
This is my life
And my soul I give raw,
I'll show me myself
If you won't forget what you saw.
I need you to love me,
And to love what I do,
To let me sink inside myself
And, then, be born anew.
From inside of my shell
Where failure makes less of me,
I give you these words
Out of desperate necessity.

Never Told

Inside this cave
You call your soul,
Echoes the hurt,
Desperation never told.
You can hear your heart beat
And feel the blood flow,
But reflections in the mirror
Reveal someone
You do not know.
You call out for someone,
As if to be so bold.
Now, your screaming in rage
Desperation never told.
It sounds off in your hollows
And returns inside of you,
You can feel it as it swallows
As your whole becomes few.
Lost in its cavity,
Every breath you take is cold.
The loudest silence
You've ever heard,
Desperation never told.

On Sunset

Sitting against the glass
Of the coffee shop,
Three hours past noon.
Silence inside my head
As my eardrums popped,
At the sight of you.
And you glowed from the inside
And my heart stopped,
You were bright as the moon.
Then you smiled
And I was sent to heaven's very top,
I was brand new.
I was carried away
As I burned white hot,
With indecent thoughts of you.
Dying to get started
So I could tell you to stop,
Not hoping that you do.
It was the fourth but you were my first
As you touched a virgin spot,
I knew.
That it was you and I
Ready or not
When on Sunset,
I met you.

Phantom Limb

You are a part of me
Even though you are not there,
You do not lay beside me
My burdens
You do not bare.
I go without you
Yet inside me
You still move,
I feel you with me
Yet, your presence
I cannot prove.
The blood that runs through you
Runs through my own veins,
And even though
You are physically misplaced
Your hollowed spot remains.
You have become my second nature
You are my way in the dark,
You can touch what is far from me
And through your skin
I can feel the beat of my own heart.
You are my love
And my life
All of the dreams within,
You are the reason

You are the change
You are my phantom limb.

Reflections

Upon reflections
I see this girl
And she is every bit of me,
And although she's grown
And has traveled far
She is still so easy to see.
I grab her hand
And she smiles at me
In a way to say hello,
And just as old friends
I smile back
At this girl
That I still know.
We sit and chat
About the days
Back when we were one,
About the tears
That flooded our ocean dreams
And the stolen moments
When we had fun.
We talked about how far I've come
And how far
I had yet to go,
But beyond her eyes
I could see
She wasn't saying

What I should know.
All in time is all she said
Before she waived good bye,
And out of my reflections
Back into myself
Is where she goes to lie.
And from her wisdom
I was born
The way I am today,
And she'll be back
To talk some more
When she needs
To show me the way.
And at every point
Within my life
Where there are choices
I must select,
I will take the time
To call on her
And together
We will always reflect.

Sing

I wish that I could sing
Because then
I'd say this with a song,
But all I have are these words
Yet I doubt they could do much wrong.
And I can't carry a note
But there's a melody
Between these lines,
And if I felt
You knew their meaning
I'd say them a thousand times.
And even if I managed to hum
It still wouldn't be the same,
Because nothing is sweeter
In or out of my mouth
Than the savor of your name.
I wish that we could sing together
But somehow
I'm always off key,
Except for that silent song you sing
When you are laying
Next to me.
And it will never be recorded
Or sold to millions
But still it's worth much more,
So that when you sing

In front of them
I know it's us
You're singing for.

Still

I think I still love you
But I'm not really sure,
Shouldn't I demand more of myself
And ask for so much more?
Should I follow
My very first thoughts,
Or rather should I listen
To my infinite heart of hearts.
I think I still feel
Something inside,
But yet I feel as if
Something has died,
Like every time we yelled
Like every time I cried.
I think I love you
But still I'm not sure,
Don't know how to say this
Or what I'm saying this for.
I think I love you
Not sure still,
One day I'll know
One day you will.

Tell Him

How do you tell a man
That you have only just met
That you have loved him
All of your life,
That in your mind
From that very first moment,
You were already
His adoring wife.
That he may not be aware
But you have already shared
Over and over
A kiss,
In all of your dreams
Both day and night
You two have lived
In eternal bliss.
How do you tell him
That in your nights apart
Your body is overwrought by pain,
That without him it seems
Your summers freeze
And your sunshine
Is only rain.
Your heart is his
And your mind never wonders

Too far from thoughts of his face,
And everywhere
You go without him
To you
Is a lonely place.
How do you tell him
All of these things
When you have just said
Your first hellos,
Or is it that
There's no need to speak
Of things he already knows.

Tell You

I tell you of things
That are of me,
In ways that are real
To touch
To see.
Tangible loves,
Fears and sorrows,
Painting a vision
Of future todays
And of yesterday's tomorrows.
I give of myself
In complete dimensions,
To ease the pressure
Loosening the tie of tensions.
I deliver in form
Not all will understand,
Summoning brilliance,
Making it work
On command.
Feel me in these words,
Between the lines
On this page,
My heart bleeds now
On my paper
My stage.
Ask if I love it

And I very well do,
Ask it of me
Poetically
I will tell you.

The Wrath

Feel the wrath
And the components
Of your demise,
Feel yourself fall
Watch my grace as I rise.
Like smoke from the fire
I escape you,
Like fuel to the flame
I shall make you.
Burn with contempt
And digest the poison
Of this serpentine,
Be swallowed by the revenge
Of which you fiend.
For whatever evil you throw
Lands back in your hands,
Be a slave to your wishes
And a product of your commands.
So in the sweat of your fear
Take this shallow bath,
Be surrounded by your faults
And drown
In the wrath.

They Forget

How soon they forget
Yet how quickly they remember,
No one cares who you are today
But are intrigued by last September.
People live and people die
But in between they change,
And even some get tangled in
Life's messy, rugged mange.
But I am one
Who made it out,
Even after you clipped my wings.
I am one who flew to God
From the ashes of evil things.
And soared through turbulent storms
Only to be washed clean,
These are things you will not remember;
A voyage unrecorded or seen.
For the most indestructible powers
Are the ones you cannot touch,
And the memories you hold on to
Are the ones that don't matter much.
And to think I was almost lost
Remembering my ruin and rot,
And by the graces was saved
By birth given strengths
That I had somehow forgot.

Within

And where do I start,
How can I begin
To tell you about myself,
These demons within.
I am who you fear,
Everything
From which you try to hide,
I am the secrets you tell;
I am the barren soil inside.
And when you hold back the tears,
I am the one who wipes them dry.
I am the truth
They can't see behind your lie.
And when you turn your back,
I am still facing you,
And when you want to be alone
I am the one who makes us two.
When you run away from them,
It is to me that you run
And when you erase the weight of guilt,
I am the one who returns a ton.
When you throw yourself to the floor,
I am the one on which despair falls
And when you're afraid to leave your
room,
It's because I am the one

Who roams the halls.
To know who I am
First dig inside your soul,
Gather your broken pieces
And once again become whole.
And that's where I start,
And that's where I begin,
From what you know about yourself,
From all your demons within.

Woman

She is a woman
In every sense of the word.
So strong in her convictions,
She makes her every thought
Heard.
She is a woman
And she knows
This is true,
As she bares every pain
That has been spared unto you.
And at times,
She will sacrifice
Even a comfortable life,
To fight for her beliefs
And all she deems as right.
And for those who cast stones
With intensions
To crucify,
She welcomes
One chance at truth
Alongside
A thousand chances to die.
She is a woman,
At the curve of her waist,
At the tenderness of her thigh,
At the plump of her breasts

And at her head's incline.
Here she stands,
Still a woman,
Whether naked or dressed.
Here she stands,
Cooking and cleaning,
Caring
Without rest.
And no one who has touched her
Can change that fact;
No amount of penetration
Can permeate
Her spiritual tact.
She is a woman,
Since the beginning of time;
She cannot be counted as coins,
As a nickel or dime.
She has been given a name
Ordained by the most high
And that name is
Woman
And woman
am
I.

22504333R00034

Made in the USA
Lexington, KY
01 May 2013